| Liza Achilles

TWO NOVEMBERS

Beltway
EDITIONS

TWO NOVEMBERS

A MEMOIR OF LOVE 'N' SEX IN SONNETS

Liza Achilles

Beltway
EDITIONS

Published by Beltway Editions, 4810 Mercury
Drive, Rockville, Maryland 20853. All rights
reserved. No part of this book may be
reproduced without the publisher's written
permission, except for brief quotations in reviews.

www.beltwayeditions.com

Printed in the United States of America
10 9 8 7 6 5 4 3 2 1

Book design: Jorge Ureta Sandoval
Author photo: Clay Blackmore
Cover art: iStock, goodmoments
ISBN: 978-1-957372-11-2

Beltway Editions (www.beltwayeditions.com)
4810 Mercury Drive
Rockville, MD 20853
Indran Amirthanayagam: Publisher
Sara Cahill Marron: Publisher

Two Novembers is a recollection of true events
in the author's life. Many individuals' identifying
characteristics have been changed to respect their
privacy. Quotations have been altered to fit the
rhythm and rhyme scheme.

To whom is this one dedicated, dear?
Read on!—and I shall make that very clear.

Sonnet 1

When Reston's thick, hot, muggy and alight,—
Or rain is dancing,—or we've heaps of snow,—
Or dew is glist'nin',—or it's nearly night—
That's when to your workplace I like to go.
I love to run,—to strengthen,—feel brand new,—
To chat with those with aching hand or knee;—
The clinic has assistants—(kind!)—and, too,
A guy who did two push-ups, just for me.
You say, don't fret, I'll heal, I'm doing great—
(Your head 'n' beard like pumpkin caramel)—
And when I'm feeling good, you celebrate!—
No man has ever treated me so well.
If, E, your metal tool is truly charmed,
I know what I would wish, were I so armed.

Sonnet 2

Oh, crap! My life is just one big cliché,—
Like Hallmark cards,—and kitsch,—bikes built for two,—
Champagne plus fireworks on New Year's Day,—
On Labor Day, though, beers 'n' BBQ.
Some citizens of classy USA
Regard the hackneyed storyline as grand:—
They dug the high-speed L.A.P.D. chase
And when Jen Aniston secured the man.
But when I watched such scenes, I felt so tired.
(Are TV viewers stoned?—Rx'd?—just lit?)
Were I a woman who, instead, aspired
To do all that society thinks fit,
I'd gamely cross this off my bucket list:—
I love my physical—(ach!)—therapist!

Sonnet 3

What am I thinking?—iambs, rhymes?—a mess!
My hope behind these sonnets—I can see!—
Is futile. What, I'm aiming to impress
A star of basketball with poetry?
I neither know nor care who has the ball!
Pentameter is not your thing! However,
Perhaps we're not so diff'rent, after all:
For as I sit here, strugg'ling to be clever,
I work so hard, as thumps and throbs my heart!
And shooting hoops?—a classy way to court.
See, basketball, played well—it is an art.
And poetry of love?—a ballsy sport.
If leaping for some ball is what you do,
Well, I—dear jock—am chasing after two.

Sonnet 4

You say I'm a perfectionist:—that's true.
Idealized forms I ferret for;—that's why
I'm, champ'ion, 'specially pursuing you.
But since you're so unrivaled, how can I—
A fretful, pummeled emu—then expect
Such excellence to find his match in me?
My hands and arms?—impaired. My psyche?—wrecked
And only half rebuilt. And yet,—you see,
A better poet I'm than good ol' Shakes!
I need no flashy logic this to prove;—
Your bending your kind ears is all it takes:
This line alights upon not love!—but you've,
By now, conceded I have one more skill:—
Je t'aime as no bard has . . . or does . . . or will.

Sonnet 5

Of all the many skills to me you've taught—
Like how to mouse and type again, lift weights,
Use ice or, other times, make muscles hot
And rest whenever pain exacerbates—
The most impressive, unexpected lesson
You gave me?—how to be strong mentally.
(Look, anyone who sniggers:—I ain't messin'.)
Thus, W—then—W—E—D?—
That's what I ask myself whenever I'm
Low, lost—or near locked up! If you've deceived
This naif—(if your flirting's minor crime,—
And you'd not mind or even feel relieved
If in your training program I don't stay)—
I learned this stunt from you:—I'll be okay.

Sonnet 6

Love:—love I've stumbled into! Praise the gods!
I've all my life sought passion's witchery!
When twangs in Cupid's arrow, it defrauds
Poor victims of all sane-like normalcy!
Whereas, in cooler days, this woman used
To be, well, sort of, halfway dignified,—
She's like a mad hen now, who lacks a roost;—
Who's laying eggs already boiled and fried;—
Whose throat trills—(in your presence!)—like a frog's;—
Whose ardency's so noxious—(as you, prince,
My shoulder touch)—it conjures psychic fogs!
What joy, this unrequited hurt!—ah, since
What topic else—do tell!—what theme in hell—
Would serve for versifying half as well?

Sonnet 7

Hey doc, what's in your metal instrument?
I mean the one you use on patients' arms,
When they, like me, have accident'ly rent
Their tendons—(ouch!)—and need those magic charms
That somehow live inside that stainless steel.
Its shape is kind of rounded, like a bow;—
When rubbed on muscles—(not too hard!)—they heal
Not just because of physics—(as you know)—
But also properties so mystical,
That when you wave it, good vibes flow and when
With it anoint my skin, I wax so full:—
Imbued! Oh!—I've been sanctified again.
No other tool—or touch—could feel this grand—
(O saint!)—except for one. I'd slip my hand—

Sonnet 8

Coach dearest, why'd you hit on me so hard?
Because it's good for business? If your clients
Become attached to you—(you're no retard)—
You'll snag more cash;—now that's good market science.
Or was your ego starving—lusting!—for
Some dope, not caring if you smashed a heart?—
Flirtation is your chosen drug?—at core
You're cruel? Or did you write this in my chart:—
"Presented with self-doubt. Excessive fear.
But confidence in one domain just might
Spawn confidence within another sphere.
Experiment with come-ons." Or—(my knight!)—
Do you me really like,—I mean, legit?—
And think me cute?—and sweet?—nah, that's not it.

Sonnet 9

Back when I was a lonely, awkward girl,
I wished to emulate an elder skilled
At navigating life, who would unfurl
The abstruse mysteries of how to build
A loving home and laudable career
And how to make the world a nicer place.
This mentor was elusive, until—dear!—
Some decades on, I saw your gingered face.
Whereas, before, I used to think, "I'll act
Like so-and-so, but with this caveat,"
Now I wholeheartedly—without redact—
Attempt to be like you:—that says a lot!
But there's one small impediment. You see,
You're male. As woman, how am I to be?

Sonnet 10

You said, "I trust you," peering in my eyes,—
Referring to my copyediting
Of your brochure—your plan to advertise:—
An innocent remark!—or so it seemed.
So then, I typed, "Yours (truly)," clicking Send,—
Alluding to your capture of my heart:—
A risky, not so blameless email's end.
(As always, I'm the dubious upstart,
While you continue stainless as a god.)
But, please, let me explain. I am so good
That angels can't compete, I swear! Applaud—
I beg you, love!—this alibi:—I could
Not cheat,—not ever. Plus, I trust you, too:—
I trust that you'd not let us be untrue.

Sonnet 11

Hello, kind therapist:—I need your help.
No, sadly,—I'm not feeling well today.
I thank you, though, for asking. I've been dealt
Some chancy cards;—and yet I'll be okay
If you'll have mercy and give tender aid.
I know you will—seraphic altruist!—
If possible—(you'd muster a brigade
If someone needed one)—so here's my list:—
Will you massage this ache inside my thumb?
These weights—how many reps?—how many sets?
What if my hands start ting'ling or go numb?
Advise:—should I go longer?—should I rest?
Your bringing ice might help;—do you agree?
One more request:—will you please cum in me?

Sonnet 12

It floors me—flawlessness. Are you for real?
If you were featured in a book of fiction,
'Twould be too pat:—prepost'rous! Yet, genteel,
Sincere—that's you. When strikes muscly affliction,
Into the medical event you delve,—
Ensuring no one's sad, perturbed or tense,—
While jugg'ling therapeutic labours twelve—
(Like Hercules!)—with stunning confidence.
"All ways perfection he's," I told my shrink,
Who scornfully—(I ditched her quick)—replied:—
"All people have defects! What did you think?"
If that's the truth, your flaw might be you eyed
My bod,—plus, you're a flirt;—is that your dirt?
If so, please tell me, sweetie:—who was hurt?

Sonnet 13

Unfortunately, sweet, we've never kissed;—
Exchanged we haven't lovey-dovey words.
When we don't meet, I don't know,—was I missed?
Nor have we hiked through woods or spotted birds.
Not once have I watched basketball you play.
You've seen me on a treadmill—within walls—
But never gard'ning on a bright, clear day;—
Nor have I seen your kids serve tennis balls.
I'd love to sit with you when night creeps in
And brush my mended hand along your cheek;—
But this I've never done, nor hugged your skin,
Nor woken warm beside your—(hot!)—physique.
Why do I smile and laugh, despite such dearth?—
I'm grateful you—(like me!)—exist on earth.

Sonnet 14

"Obsessive," "worrywart," "brain's full of cheese,"
"A basket case," "hysteric," "off her rocker"—
A wise one, rightly, could pronounce I'm these;—
In error, though, they'd be to dub me "stalker."
How, then, know I your age and where you live?
Well, duh,—you aired your birth year, month and date
To tell some story—(babe, you're talkative!)—
And, doc, my first appointment, you were late:—
"Yikes! Where's he coming from?" I gasped, to learn.
I won't try to attend—(you think I'm mad?!)—
Your practices or games—(I'll only yearn)—
Nor trail your car, nor peek—(def not!—egad!)—
At night, through leaves, into your windowpane.
Fine, call me "nuts"!—just know, in this, I'm sane.

Sonnet 15

I, nervous, patient, in your clinic stand,
Begin—(I'm craving luck:—a four-leaf clover)—
To ask you something and keep talking, and
You rise! *I'm av'rage height;—you tower over!*
I finish doing sit-ups. You stroll near,
Peer down and drawl:—words playful, wise 'n' lovely.
I laugh! You smile. (Oh, I could use a beer.)
I'm lying on the floor;—you are above me!
I'm feeling sore from push-ups done last week.
I tell you, "I've a hurt inside my chest."
You show me where! (I somehow do not freak.)
You graze your finger just above my breast!
You've graced me with no crystal, vow or clue.
No hope—(sigh)—should I have. *And yet I do!*

Sonnet 16

Hi hon. Are you still reading these poor rhymes?
Still sitting in your chair? (Falling asleep?)
Imbibing this grand epic of our times?—
Or not? (You dumped this in the garbage heap?)
If lucky moons do shine, you are still turning
The pages of this little book. If true,
I wonder whether they have left you burning
To tenderly reciprocate your view.
If so, perhaps you're pacing, feeling nerves.
"I'm not a poet!" cry you in alarm.
Don't fret! I don't expect from you a verse;—
Would you ask me to treat an injured arm?
My expertise?—I lay down lines all phat.
Dear, yours is physicality:—use that!

Sonnet 17

My handsome sage:—if stars and Halley's comet
You wanted,—them I'd bring you on a dish.
Just kidding—(didn't mean to make you vomit)—
I can't do that;—and who'd have such a wish?
Now, if you wanted me to pack your lunch,
Well, that's for real! I'd feed you veggies fresh.
If, though, you had a hankering to munch
On chips, I'd ziplock handfuls. To refresh
You when you finished work, I'd rub your feet
And big, strong shoulders. If you have to view
The Final Four to make your life complete,
I'll buy, sports fan, two tix—and plane tix, too!
But, if your greatest yearning is to banish
This gal from any contact?—k. I'll vanish.

Sonnet 18

Your woman wants a bunch of pretty flowers.
(She told me this;—I'm just the messenger.)
She said, she needs them in the next few hours,—
And only you can buy them, just for her.
She hates those artificial colored blooms,
Like white carnations dyed lime,—turquoise,—teal.
Forget, too, fake ones lacking sweet perfumes;—
You'd better go with fresh cut,—that's the deal.
It doesn't matter which bud types you choose—
(Rose?—lily?—daisy?—iris?—all okay!)—
As long as they have fragrant scents, and hues
Are vibrant—at their peak!—in this bouquet.
Next, write, "With Love," then bring it here, dear groom;—
She wants them in a vase in my front room!

Sonnet 19

I love you, coach:—but no one knows this fact.
Too, love I all my friends;—I can't share this
One datum, though:—they'd think I judgment lacked.
First, probably, they'd smirk. They'd, next, dismiss
My posit that you, doctor—(whom I pay
To tendonitis heal, build muscles and
Keep propping up morale:—"You'll be okay!")—
Are more than just a gorgeous hired hand.
This secret's cosmic, dark and threatening
To swallow me inside its vortexed grip;—
So I'm in sonnets feelings packaging:—
Thank Venus nada is my readership!
Yet:—would you think it hurtful, lame or flagrant
If—(yikes!)—I found a literary agent . . . ?

Sonnet 20

Since no one's read this poem, no one knows
I told my husband "bye" in part because
Severe health fails and mad crushing expose
What abstract contemplation seldom does.
And no one knows how cried I heartily
When I attempted to your program leave—
(I'd long before progressed past therapy)—
How quitting again last week did me grieve.
You have a wife and three children;—although
My Lexapro transmutes me less than sober,
Through haze:—you separated long ago!!!—
You shared this on this last day of October!
I couldn't take it;—don't call me a dork:—
I told my mom 'bout you. Her mouth's a cork.

Sonnet 21

Sleek, confident, cool, charismatic boy:—
Now, why are, suddenly, you acting shy?
We're staring down cascades of plumbless joy.
Two banks we're standing on, apart. It's my
Opinion that we jump, in concert, should
Into the fathomless abyss! Condone
You this, my slick and blissful plan?—or would
You rather, sitting, parched, we merely phone?!
Don't get me wrong, sweetheart;—you made my year.
On Halloween night, terribly I slept;—
No ghouls or ghosts, but memos did appear:—
You texted me! Into my phone you've leapt;—
Let's dive in deeper! Damn:—I feel like cursin'!
Highflyer, when?—will I?—see you in person?

Sonnet 22

On sleepy mornings, often, I'm perplexed:—
Did—really—x event occur?—or, dreamt
I, merely, that it happened? Digging, next,
In fresh-cached memories, I truth attempt—
In vain—to find. Then, wham!—I realize x
Is just chimeric:—false. My teeth I clean
And brew my tea, as—(like a multiplex)—
My mind replays and 'plays the spectral scene:—
With variations. If I soon live through
A like occurrence,—it's as if I've done
It twice. (Does your brain act illusive, too?)
Now, since you haunt my dreams and daydreams, hon,
This quirk of mine's a boon—an awesome service—
'Cause when we tryst "again"—I won't be nervous!

Sonnet 23

The field of medicine—(ace of a swain)—
Prescribes of healers arduous, long hours.
All day you're laying hands on those in pain,
Bestowing remedies, advice and powers.
I can relate to tough work, 'cause I used
To be a teacher:—helping teens is taxing.
I graded,—taught,—curricula produced;—
My writing gig is so much more relaxing.
Your days are filled not just with patient care;—
You also write up comprehensive notes,—
Employees manage,—haggle Medicare,—
Then, in your spare time, adolescents coach.
Star-lucky me:—you work you to the bone,
Yet carved out time to be with me—alone!!!!

Sonnet 24

On days my mood erupts and plunges down
From small frustrations, fears or serious
Dilemmas—like my love for you—I frown
And get to work:—by writing, furious.
Upon inscribing pat, creative clauses,—
I laugh aloud—ha ha!—at my own jokes
And vent my thick emotions without pauses.
Yeah, writing therapy?—it ain't no hoax.
But when the stable letters do me proud,
And tripping I'm—beflowered as a bird—
I've nil left to exude:—then forms a cloud
In me—till I eructate my next word!
A vicious circle? Nah, it's virtuous:—
Life's agonizing strains turn glorious!

Sonnet 25

I can't compose this sonnet. I'm too tired,—
My medication blends all thoughts to goo,—
My egghead's also spinning, sliced and wired,
Recalling last night's you-me rendezvous!
I'm early, dear, to bed—this time alone—
Though, doc, I'm sure you'll be my dreams adorning.
I'm sleeping right now—(zzz)—so don't you phone;—
I'm overjoyed you did:—sunshine, it's morning!
Less scrambled since I'm now, I'll hereby note:—
Your body's stunning! Glad you like mine, too.
Your touch was strong and gentle:—all I'd hoped;—
The more we loved, the more I cherished you.
I've guessed, I trust, what your reply will be:—
How 'bout we meet again, next time you're free?

Sonnet 26

Your business has a Twitter page:—I scrolled.
I found there—(lo!)—of you an ugly snapshot.
I scowled at you, but knew the file was gold:—
I saved it to the desktop of my laptop.
A month ago this was. I have, since then,
Beheld you nearly every day. You look
So weary in this photo—(downtrodden,—
Bags under eyes)—as if you undertook
Too much the day before,—slept not enough.
Despite, though, feeling drained, you're smiling slightly:—
As always, striving to excel,—be tough.
This image—whereas—(sorry!)—I unsightly,
For weeks, thought—(handsome!)—it to partake of,—
I now see in your blue eyes purely love.

Sonnet 27

I gifted you brown eggs;—you made an omelette.
I gave tomatoes,—peppers,—cucs:—you ate 'em.
A hat—if I crocheted one—yep, you'd don it.
"Fresh goji berries, tart!"—you didn't hate 'em.
Despite my setbacks, heard I never, "See ya!"
I made a lame-ass joke;—you smiled, kind.
You said it wasn't dumb—my wack idea.
When cried I, "You can oust me!" you declined.
I baked chip-chocolate cookies:—you partook.
You could've tossed my cartoon art;—instead,
You framed it. Sonnet 1 in this li'l book
I—scared—bequeathed. You liked!—or so you said.
You're so magnanimous, how can I know
If something's fab,—or you just made it so?

Sonnet 28

Elusive redhead:—life, I know, is hard.
I'm willing to endure adversity
Because I know no human went unscarred,—
Not even those, like you, who seem to be.
While—(true!)—we trysted twice within three weeks—
(Such long weeks)—I could last for months without
You touching,—feeling;—I'd slog up the peaks
Of eating,—sleeping,—heartbeating:—no doubt.
Hm,—seems into your rooms I can't just jaunt.
More presents, then, I'd like—(I'm pretty scrappy)—
To give. "I'm here for you. What do you want?"
Cried I. You answered sadly, "Just be happy."
Say jingles ring—my phone's from me four feet—
And "E" glows?—here's a gift:—yay! I'm upbeat!

Sonnet 29

There seems to be a wee small disconnect
Between our meeting minds—(if nothing else!)—
'Cause our relationship—hon, I'd expect
The two of us to give it lifts and helps.
Important is the sex to you;—me, too.
But deep, long conversations aren't your style?
And "Just the facts, ma'am"—that's the way you do?
Your bestest space is on some mancave isle?
To give you credit, dear:—for time you're hurting;—
Work, sleep and fam'ly take priority.
That's good. But—(really?!)—you deny your flirting?
You're merely nice?—just liked to work with me?
Ye changeling species, men! What's your jujitsu?
Stud? Lover? Alien? . . . I just don't get you!

Sonnet 30

My darling bee:—I know that you are busy;—
Is bzzzyness your cause of scarcity?
More causes are there? (Though it makes me dizzy
To scope your brain,—I'll strive to nail that sea.)
What other squalls are trying you to weather
That might explain your entering regress?
(Ironic it's that, now that we're together,
Exchange we intel with each other less.)
Do you feel guilty? Why? We didn't cheat.
You think legalities apply? They don't.
My poem irked you? (Ain't hip 'nuff this beat?)
Are you afraid I'll ditch yo' ass? I won't!
I'd like to talk. Will you do me this favor?
I won't ask much. (Just one night more to savor. . . .)

Sonnet 31

Olympic flame:—there's nothing wrong with you.
Your light's as bright as winter's yuletide tree:—
A star—(wise sovereigns follow,—not just view)—
Of psychological sagacity.
While clash I with dark demons—(daily screaming
Inside my head)—your struggle's opposite;—
Whereas I feel too much, your circuits—gleaming—
Run logically and smoothly and with grit.
Although you think you love me not so much,
I sense you do!—but hate, more, murky haze.
You felt abandoned as a kid?—now clutch
Your lustrous backbone?—I tend my own blaze!
You're thus a brilliant, lone, unlonely wolf?
I'll be your moon. Let us the night engulf.

Sonnet 32

For months, an itch within my palm harassed me.
I scratched and scratched and scratched!—to no avail.
You took my hand and gently bent it backly;—
This healing act my tick'ling did curtail.
For years, I yearned to 'cquire a wiser head.
I read and read!—but still felt lost, unsaved.
But when observed I boons you did and said,
Your sapience supplied the lessons craved.
For decades, longed to sleep I with a man
Who, when a woman's confident, a bitch
He doesn't think her,—who's a hottie—and
Whom I adore. (I did!) But, damn, that itch—
It, strangely, has returned. Those urges, too.
Let's do it all again—sweet—me and you!

Sonnet 33

[The gender modes of our society
Are binding, omnipresent and bizarre.]
(One.) Girls are taught our sexuality
Is dangerous,—our bodies we must guard.
(Two.) She is trained to passively heed him.
(Three.) Sex for shiny things she's told to barter;—
For fucks, indulge he's s'pposed to every whim:—
The more she wants, his work is that much harder.
[Now, sexism—it cuts both ways, you guys.]
(Three.) I don't wish to trade my love for loot.
It's free to have, for you I rhapsodize.
Since, wouldn't our romance be poor and moot
If founded on consumerism? (More
I've penned on this:—see sonnet 34.)

Sonnet 34

(I thus proceed from sonnet 33.)
I'll buy myself my dinner, jewelry, shows.
Yet, if you freely give, I'll graciously
Accept;—no ban on presents I'll impose.
But:—you're reluctant our relationship
To nurture, 'cause you're not sure you can give.
(Two.) Here I can't be timid. I won't gyp
Me out of paradise. Screw modes, I'll live
Assertively;—I'll active be! I'll tell
You straight:—there's nothing, love, I want, except
To see you, proffer you gifts, treat you well—
(Expressing such—remember, heart?—I wept)—
And, lastly, (One.) go with you all the way.
[We both will see advantage thusly,—eh?]

Sonnet 35

You told me, beautiful, that girls freak out
When you reveal you cannot give too much.
"I nothing want," I voiced and did not pout
Or beg for mawkish language, gifts and such.
"That's new," you said, confused at my reply.
My words, though, weren't precise, because I had
One meager plea:—"We'll meet again?" peeped I.
"As time permits," said you, "to I'd be glad."
Next thing I know, apologizing you're
For never granting me a date;—you say
You nothing feel. I counter, "Though no whore
Am I,—no strings attached, I'll with you lay!"
You're cool with that—(me, too!)—till you time out:—
You secrets loathe. Ah, now who's freaking out?

Sonnet 36

Is it because you healed me, medic dear?—
Is that the reason for my adoration?
I, like a sick or wounded grenadier,
The carer worship who dispensed salvation?
Or is it 'cause male power turns me on?
They say three waves of feminism hit;—
Despite them, lusted I to be your pawn,
When on all fours you ordered me to get!
You'd never make—('course not!)—such a command,
Were it not in the service of my health—
(To teach a workout)—so it's 'cause you stand
On morals?—i.e., goodness is your wealth?
Just this I know:—you could be Waterloo,—
And still, for Christmas, all I'd 'tempt is you.

Sonnet 37

I'm overwhelmed in this pre-holiday,—
This time of rushing 'round to every store;—
I've barely time to sleep,—I've bills to pay,—
Yet still I'm adding debt,—'cause I want more!
I bought some winter clothes, a bed, a pillow,
Replacement windows, gin and powdered sugar.
I'm planning to stay warm when we get real snow
But mainly hoping you'll think, "She's a looker!"
If spotting me in my pink gloves, red sweater
Or black-and-white p.j.'s;—and you'll be cozy
If sleeping here;—and you'll enjoy life better
If eating baked goods frosted loving-slowly!
All week, in shops and kitchen, thus I toiled.
I cookies sent. You called me! (I'm so spoiled!)

Sonnet 38

I—calm, collected, but too foggy—chose
To slash the dose of my antidepressant.
I feel much better!—till my ancient foes
Resume their bantering and goads incessant.
They urge me, "Lift more weight with both your arms!"
I overdo it. Laugh they, "Nyah, you're injured!"
I, panicked, text you, "These muscular harms—
How do I, P.T., heal them?!" But you're hindered
From answering, 'cause soon I'm blushing while
Explaining, "False alarm! I need no aid, boss!
I upped my dose;—I once again can smile."
You barely notice!—have your own life's chaos:
At first, it's "Only sex!" Now, "Only talk!"
It's not just me who's wishy-washy, doc!

Sonnet 39

Some poems back, I stated that I think
You're—in a wolflike, philophobic way—
Real fond of me. Before I use more ink
Extolling our intrigue, I want to say,
I shouldn't!—so I won't!—assume you love
This sad, amour-afflicted gal—or will.
However, babe, I fit you like a glove;—
Your wish to be heard,—heeded I fulfill.
Since you appear to love my company,
Perhaps I'm by you wholly lovable;—
Perhaps that complicated tapestry—
(Your life)—necessitates a months-long mull.
If there's a chance you'll upgrade me from "nice"
And "sexy" to "belov'd,"—I'll roll the dice.

Sonnet 40

I—this upcoming year—resolve to read
More books than finished I the past twelve months.
I'll get in shape. My instincts I will heed
When making big and small decisions. Once
I make some home improvements, I'll invite
Friends frequently to pass the time with me,
And, therefore, I commit to fix that light,
Paint, organize and clean. I vow to see
My family more often,—keep my brothers
Looped in:—their state from here, alas, is far.
I pledge to be as courteous to others—
Yet powerf'ly assertive—as you are.
And if I can—in any way—help you
Keep all your covenants,—I'll do that, too.

Sonnet 41

I miss your bod. I scheme incessantly
To get so I might lounge—(luxuriate!)—
Within the same hotel room, therapy
Outpatient treatment center, real estate
Possessed by you or me or party else,
Car, tent or cave as you. Remember I
This fondly:—I curled up petite dumbbells—
As, in the chest machine, you raised on high—
(Enthroned there!)—nearly the full stack of weights.
And this:—I hopped the hip adductor strut
And toward the tables glanced—to learn the Fates
Had spun you'd be massaging some girl's butt.
To bunk by you, must I induce pain chronic?—
A brilliant plan!—if I were that moronic.

Sonnet 42

You say you won't be free for eight long years.
When you've made resolutions, you them keep,
Regardless of your cravings;—without tears
You climb up steadily your road so steep.
Penelope as well as faithful Argos,
The wife and dog—(know you your classic lit?)—
Of he who traveled 'round the sea the farmost,
For twenty years their vigil did not quit.
At last, received he from his gal a smooch—
Odysseus, who seemed a beggar, staff
In hand,—though I feel sorry for the pooch.
Achilles, doubtlessly, can less than half
That time abide. A way to?—I'll unearth it.
Eight years?—that's nothin', babe!—because you're worth it.

Sonnet 43

Am I the only straight girl chasing you?
Ex-therapist, can it be true that I'm
Your only former patient/trainee who
Saw sensible, mad sexiness each time
She hobbled in to be treated or trained?—
Or did one see—but judge you are too hot—
(Out of her league,—not feasibly attained)—
And prob'ly taken? This, myself, I thought!—
Till, through some transcendental combination
Of sluggish dawning of my worthiness
Of being cherished and your validation
Of my edging toward healing, strength and bliss,—
I saw into your life I me might weave.
(That's why it's key to listen,—hope,—believe.)

Sonnet 44

I texted:—"Want to meet for dinner,—drinks?
I'll pay. You pick the day." Next, with elation,—
I sent good news. You texted back—(ah, sphinx)—
Congrats!—but you ignored the invitation.
I handwrote you a card:—inside, I drew
Cute, cartoon animals—'n' asked once more.
You called to thank me—(graciously, it's true)—
Yet mentioned nothing 'bout a date. Therefore,
I emailed:—"Hey, how 'bout I bring up booze
And food tomorrow?" Sweet, you wrote right back—
Discussing other matters. I don't lose,
Nor win;—guess I'll keep play'n' my beggar track.
Heart,—think you that success arrives by dint
Of dogged trials?—or can't I take a hint?

Sonnet 45

My demons—on the loose again—are saying
False, wild and nasty things about you, hon:
According to their chorus, you've been preying
On my sensitive temperament, for fun.
It suited you just fine—our two-night stand,
But further hooking up would be—(they sneer)—
Indulgent, since you of yourself demand
A stoic life,—'xcept when from it you veer.
You crave my body, but my brain annoys:—
When I ask questions, passionate words use
Or share my close-held secrets. Classy boys
Won't tell me why,—just snub me—(they abuse)—
But as they kept on screaming—inhumane—
I snuck out:—fled cross-country on a plane!

Sonnet 46

When those cruel, raucous voices visit me—
(I, fortunately, unlike my forebear,
Don't actually them hear)—there's remedy
In—(dear motif!)—the subject that they air.
They rag on you;—but when you speak or write,
Your sane, concise communication style
Combats them as no blade or gunshot might—
(Were they—perhaps?—less ghoul, more crocodile)—
And thus, when I'm assailed—my mind afluster,
Distinctly rattled by each unique zero—
But suddenly receive from you—(ghostbuster!)—
An email, text or phone call—(superhero!)—
No matter if—in fetal gloom—I'm curled,—
Your language soothes:—all's right within this world.

Sonnet 47

My vacay's me injected with new pep:—
I give those imps the slip! Now, I should warn ya,
Long tales 'n' fam'ly gossip I've, 'cause, yep!—
I've just returned from Southern California.
I learned all 'bout my cousin's lager making,
My aunt's signif'cant other's complications,
My uncle's mountain home, my gram's crocheting—
And *everyone's* political persuasions.
It was such fun to catch up with the fam,
I thought, why not relocate to L.A.?
I'd oranges and lemons grow! Yeah, damn!—
Why shouldn't I bask in the warmth each day,
Espying all the stars—and how the surf breaks?—
'Cause you're, good-looker, East Coast! (Also:—earthquakes.)

Sonnet 48

Now, here's a philosophic inquiry—
For all ye folk with minds inquisitive:—
What is the meaning of a vacancy,—
That is, the absence of a substantive?
What does it signify when there's no beta
To ratify the motive alpha force?
Attempts at pinning down the unknown strata
Of worlds beyond are frequently, of course,
Not only fruitless but a waste of spunk
That could be spent on worldly games:—delights
Like Scrabble,—Twitter,—chasing you, sweet hunk!
Still, I aspire to rise to those great heights,—
To learn what it might mean when you don't call.
(I do suspect I know:—nothing at all.)

Sonnet 49

I wrote a book of fiction:—it's quite novel!
I'm—ugh—a walking advertisement of
My work. (They say—in Boston—it's a marvel!)
I'm, too, forever pitching you my love.
Each day, I email bigwigs in the city,
Attempting to entice someone to bite;—
I write you, next, a note that's sweet 'n' witty.
My phone, though, seldom dings:—not day,—not night.
I'll try, therefore, a different baiting tack:—
I'll talk to agents! Experts say one should
Be able to describe one's paperback
While moving between building floors;—if stood
We two, however, in an elevator,—
I'd clasp 'n' kiss you! (Speeches could come later.)

Sonnet 50

Since waiting's agony, if—absent guy—
I email you and agents and then—quick!—
Direct my whole attention elsewhere, I
Won't call them dimwit snobs—or you a dick.
I'll be too busy doing other stuff!—
Like, for example, writing one more note
That I can send to hook my decent, buff,
Intelligent amour, to make you dote
On me!—or one to lure some gatekeepers
Into the prosy tendrils of my book,
Until one grabs—(exclaiming, "Christ jeepers!")—
Her phone. (Will no one at me fondly look?!)
Which is more likely, hearing good news from
A lit agent?—or you—cruel, laggard bum?

Sonnet 51

Engulfed am I by emptiness. The rain
Subsides and seeps to dryness. When I think
About you, I despair. Like ice, my pain
Absconds in drops,—but only when I drink.
That doleful day for valentines—it passed—
And as I'm Pisces—(sensitive,—marine)—
My birthday did. The gifts you gave—(aghast
Am I at their brutality)—pristine
Are in their barrenness. To you return
The favor—that constrained am I to do.
So when your birthday pops around, I'll burn
No candles,—send no ode, lay or haiku;—
Instead I'll—(since you leave me here in limbo)—
Long hair—white dress—just flit:—window to window.

Sonnet 52

I dreamt that you were cooking dinner for
Us two. I did not recognize the kitchen:—
Your digs?—where I have never been? You wore
I can't say what;—but, sweetheart, with no flinchin',
You let me hold your muscular torso—
Your bellybutton 'gainst my own—and yet
Your lips and eyes I did not see or know.
Your toil I did not offer to abet;—
Then as I waited on the carpet of
The 'djoining room, you called, "What time is it?"
"It's 6:15 a.m." Though somehow, love,
We'd not yet ate, I did not mind a bit.
And then my ex appeared!—with darkened brow!
"I thought you had a girlfriend!" "I do *now*!"

Sonnet 53

The season:—shamrocks, snow and basketball.
The mood:—wild alternation 'tween the poles.
Some luck?—yeah, I would take it, price and all—
(As Bruce shouts)—and thus justify my goals.
This wintry mix?—so rare this year, strangely.
Just yesterday I wore a short-sleeved shirt—
Emblazoned by my university—
And wasn't cold. They played so well!—assert
I, though I know not much about the game.
'Specia'ly that long, smooth, arced, coop'rative
Dunk shot I liked. You might think this is lame:
My driveway had a forlorn hoop. Forgive
Me, love:—I spun it right, installed a net
And bought a ball. 'Cause you I can't forget.

Sonnet 54

Enchanter:—one whole moon it's been since I
Dispatched you news;—you answered me with silence.
Since clear, direct intel's in short supply,
I'm forced to turn to mystic hints for guidance:—
I've, heart, a superstition 'bout a song
They sometimes play on local radio;—
Too, prides of particles unite us strong-
Ly, bypassing our distance. This these show:—
You long to see me—but, more, wish to shield
Your life, that's set, from flops and take the high way.
I thirst to tell you that my arms have healed
So beautif'ly, I shoveled my whole driveway!—
That said I, when a man romanced me, "No."—
But—I intuit—you already know.

Sonnet 55

You're your own boss!—but did ever endure
You higher-ups who shat upon your dreams?
One time, in scorn and fear of lit'rature,
My supervisor threw away bound reams
Of Bradstreet, Dickinson, Thoreau and Frost,
On purpose so I couldn't teach those masters
To high schoolers. These kids, she griped, are lost;—
And idealistic teachers spawn disasters.
At night, I'd fantasize about her head:—
I'd smash it!—*craaack!* Today, I itch the faces
To bash of my rejecters!—but, instead,
I scrawled these fourteen lovely, lilting traces
All 'bout the delicacy of a bluebell
In springtime. (I mean, come on, can't, dude, you tell?)

Sonnet 56

Head-spinner:—how shall I interpret your
Behavior when you azure wore,—when last
We met? Your Kool-Aid eyes—I did adore
How long your hair was, grazing never past
Them, so not to impound those spiked, wild beauties:—
Voracious for yours truly. Juvie chasms
Were they of termless joy. Next—(were we cuties?—
Since my look copied yours?)—enthusiasms
And questions raced! You needed not to miss
My exit:—smiling up from patients, "Bye!—
Good day!—All health!" cried you. Was all of this
Mere pose?! Regardless—twice, not once!—got I—
(Nobody can take this away from me)—
Laid by the suavest babe in all P.T.

Sonnet 57

Could we have ended any other way?
Reality is more hardwired to
Prosaism than each absurd foray
Of my imagination. Misconstrue
Scenarios I often, 'cause when there's
An information shortage, my machine
Fills all the gaps with either crude nightmares—
Or fantasies of me as winsome queen.
I know my flaws;—and so, "Don't sugarcoat
Your answer," texted I, "but blurt, outright!—
A yea or nay." You still declined to vote.
I know your style's exception'ly polite;—
But silence throws construal up to chance!—
And risks ensuing awkward circumstance. . . .

Sonnet 58

Sooo, I showed up, with no forewarning, late,—
To find out what would happen. Would you steer
Me through the door?—or smile and take the bait?
"L, whatcha need?" "I don't know why I'm here!"
Sooo, spoke I with your patient,—your assistant,
The TVs watched and teased you with a grin, "It's
'Bout time for ice!" Meh. You were sullen,—distant.
"I'm busy after." "Please:—can I've two minutes?"
You strode where none was. Sooo, I'd hoping been
To stay till you got off!!—but I you tailed.
You mumbled, ". . . honest . . ."—kept on stammerin',
"I mean. . . ." You mean—*my poetry has failed?!!!*
Next day, I emailed:—"Sorry! Thanks! I'll scat."
"For understanding, thanks." And that is that.

Sonnet 59

Since you're—(alas!)—no more my lover boy,
I swam through murky online dating waters:—
Most men more faith than I have, act so coy
They don't post squat or hope we'll be globetrotters.
But one's virtues include an age and height
Exceeding mine,—the absence of a void
Where photos go,—a writing style polite
And strong. He's sporty,—local,—self-employed:—
Hm,—just like you! We talked an hour 'n'a half.
Good grief!—this man is bright, exuberant,
Articulate and sweet—and makes me laugh.
A braggart?—nah, he's blithely confident.
Yet:—this near zero means. To meet's to see—
(A watershed!)—how flows our chemistry?

Sonnet 60

Sweet muse:—if ever you decide to venture
Online to seek a girlfriend, lay or soulmate,—
You might wonder what to display v. censure
In that grand quest to fascinate your goal date.
Here are some tips, then, from a gal's perspective:
If you upload no pic, she'll—(sorry!)—bet
You look like Grendel's mother. More effective?—
Say cheese!—as you work out—or hug your pet.
Your profile should detail abundant passions,—
And—(trust me, 'cause I've spent many a day there)—
Your first note should be not too slaved to fashions,—
Yet classier—and longer—than just "Hey there."
Now,—if some fellow does all this just right,
I prob'ly won't reject him,—though I might!

Sonnet 61

Shall I describe to you a summ'ry guy?
He is more lovely and more temperate
Than one Fair Youth, who, long ago, did die,—
Forgot by all not taking English Lit.
Superbly fits his trim, athletic frame
In jeans,—blue button-down,—black leather jacket.
Blue—(too!)—his eyes are. Men set me aflame
When older:—well, gray hair—he doesn't lack it!
On our first date, imbibed he just one stout.
He talks enough—and listens well. The joint
Has sweet potato fries, which I did tout;—
Them cheerily he ordered. At what point
Do I—oh man, and go out on a limb!—
Address a poem not to you—but him?

Sonnet 62

I guess I'm lucky: Coach, it must be rare
To Smile at some man lumped in your first set
Of Matches—your first day logged in—and fare
So famously, you're thrilled to have him met.
I guess I'm awesome: 'Soon as home I got
The brew'ry from, I emailed him:—confessed
I'd date him 'gain;—before he read my thought,
He, meanwhile, texted and the same expressed.
I guess I'm hopeful: When we both arrived
And as we left, we hugged—a duple bliss—
And truly—doctor friend—I'll feel deprived
If, on our second date, we share no kiss.
I guess I'm high: The more I chirped my song,—
The less you echoed;—his calls?—prompt and long.

Sonnet 63

Hey doc:—I have a question;—it's important.
My chirpy pal—(i.e., that dude who's fun,—
Ebullient,—verbose,—in no way dormant)—
His hockey league—(his team a cup just won!)—
Competes inside an ice house halfway 'tween
His place and mine, and for our second date,
He wants to take me skating there. I'm green
At all white, silver, wintry sports:—ice skate
I've done but rarely. Think you it's too risky?—
I might fall 'pon these two frail arms. I find
My injury has mostly healed;—but it's, see,
Not clear I'm ready for—Wait, never mind!
Forget my question, since I'll undercut
Your verdict:—going I'm, no matter what!

Sonnet 64

Dear P.T. friend,—since recently I gave
You insights from a woman's P.O.V.,
Will you—(I know I'm on thin ice)—please waive
Your reticence and do the like for me?
My quand'ry:—I had been, the week before
I met that gray one—(here's a tame subplot)—
Texts writing to a tech whiz. Since adore
I did—and do!—that skater, I could not—
In good faith—build on this IT guy's hints
On bookstores, coffeeshops and wineries.
He, ten days later, wrote again. I winced—
Yet felt no int'rest;—I can't all folks please—
And long to see what will with "Chirps" ensue:—
Should I explain myself?—or do like you?

Sonnet 65

Ex-muse:—my latest love questing's been easy.
That hot entrepreneur—(with me he clicks!)—
Me treated to beers,—salad,—pizza cheesy:—
It was a piece of (cheese)cake. Hours six
We spent in full concordance—that bright day—
The Easter skies were blue,—choreographic;—
I paused before a church:—no, not to pray,
Unless you count my cursing all the traffic
Delaying me as drove I toward the ice rink.
We smoothly circled,—dined,—prolonged our tryst
By strolling 'round the harbor. Easy—I think—
He was to be near:—cushy! (Yes, we kissed.)
Now—E—if, on date three, I satisfy—
(And entry grant)—will be too easy I?

Sonnet 66

And so, I have been making my own way,—
Not that you tendered me a choice, good doc.
Instead of ghosting that techy hombre,
I messaged why I'm out. He didn't balk
But wrote, "I 'ppreciate the honesty."
About my question in the sonnet last:—
Regardless of your view, I'm fully free
To do as I think best. If these six past
Months can be indication, I will jump
To, with a dude I like, be so unchaste
As to him squeeze, smack, snuggle, grope and hump,
As long as he will let me!—and it's safe.
Good-bye. Your muse-i-ness was all a poet
Could want. Angelic stay. Anew bestow it.

Sonnet 67

Dear F:—I'm glad your texts and emails are
Chock-full of exclamation points!!—and smiles.
I'm grateful quickly hopped you in your car;—
To care for migrained me, you traveled miles.
I'm awed you learned one of my fav'rite songs
And strummed it for me thru the phone:—so lovely.
You're hot 'n' sweet;—methinks that we's belongs
Togetha:—since you wrote the same words of me.
I'm puzzled, babe:—why don't your kisses smack?
(I'll steal 'em anyway.) You, captured, wearing
Red hockey gear?—too cute. Your nonstop yack
Keeps me—witless and tacit—from despairing.
Say one more thing I'll—quite unbashfully:—
Adore I feeling you . . . inside of me!

Sonnet 68

What were they thinking—those who manufacture
Harsh chemicals that clear the fields of weeds
But kill the honeybees? The bursting rapture
Of strawberries, fresh from my garden, feeds
My appetite like nothing else in spring;—
What are they thinking—those who grow them for
The groc'ry aisles,—their size so augmenting,
They're not too luscious—but look nice in store?
Some captain, 'cross the seas, in wood, for money,
The Asian long-horned beetle freighted;—suffer
The maples did:—what is he thinking, honey?
What was she thinking, sweet—your former lover—
When she behaved in such a way as to
Risk losing such a delicacy:—you?

Sonnet 69

Lament we:—O sick ironies of sickness.
You, worried, said, "To urgent care let's go."
I lay there shaking, sorry you should witness
My plight—as our fourth date. I told you no:—
"I'm queasy, weak, near sightless and in pain;—
How do you hope to transport me?" You fed
Me cheese and crackers,—water brought—(I'd lain
In agony four days)—and then my head
Began to clear,—my body's shiver halted,
Soon after all the nutrients ingested.
"I'm well enough to travel!" I exalted—
But didn't need to. Skinny thing, I rested.
For weight loss, ill beats diets, chanting "om"
And exercising. *Don't try this at home!*

Sonnet 70

I met a young gal who sought to reside
In my house as a tenant;—gosh, I fought the
Strong urge I had to clasp her arm and chide
Her overuse of this assertion:—"Gotcha."
A gentle lawyer friend's—(she works to fairly
Serve inmates)—stock reply is "Fair enough."
This utt'rance fits her splendidly;—too rarely
I hear it now:—to leave dear ones is tough.
I met a man who loves to tell long stories;—
Most often, you begin like this:—"It's funny, . . ."
It's funny, but those words are evening glories
I never tire of hearing. Dapper bunny:—
Have I a tic of which I'm ignorant?
Is it nerve grating?—apt?—magnificent?

Sonnet 71

Are ever—handsome duck—you in some mood?
Do you, some nights, come home from work so foul,
You seethe—or rant about how we're all screwed,—
Making your fam'ly cringe,—your doggie growl?
I can't imagine this. You're buoyed, cheerful,
Laid back and without worry,—not to mention
You love your work,—think every day's a mir'cle
In which you have great freedom of invention.
Remember I, in my own home, on eggshells
Walking, before I from that dude hightailed:
"You can't go back, veer courses or renege!" yells
My mercantile first mate:—"That ship has sailed!"
Ships sail;—it's true. But, usually, I'm on them.
All 'board!—my outlook's salty,—not just maudlin!

Sonnet 72

It's not uncanny, strange coincidence
That I got sick the very weekend that
I was to have four agents' audience:—
Five minutes to bedazzle!—or fall flat.
This is my way, you see. Whenever life
Is going great—that's when I sabotage
Myself, by introducing newfound strife
And, later, calling past success mirage.
I guess this is my way of never failing,
My subconscious perceiving any stretch
Skyward as dangerous and me derailing
Before my fall would be no simple catch.
As with my novel, so with you, sweet pea:—
Now's 'bout the time when I'll—*Don't do it, me!!*

Sonnet 73

I'd lay odds on a phone call or an email:—
So many people should be reaching out.
My ad set down my property in detail;—
Potential renters will turn up, no doubt.
I red and yellow liquid samples ceded—
A dicey gamble!—to my clinic:—please,
Luck, tell me all my worry is not needed,—
I won't lose all to some shyster disease.
I've met talk therapists in seasons prior;—
Though most of them me angered—or appalled,
Once more I'll draw some cards,—try to acquire—
Aha:—one just emailed—and also called!
Though I've increased my clicks a hundredfold,
I'll roll again—shark—for your name:—in bold!

Sonnet 74

On Tuesday night, I had two drinks of wine:—
For once, my phone-call chatter yours exceeded,
Dear graying doll. My secrets were all mine
While with my erstwhile lover. E impeded
My quirky observations not at all:—
No matter what I said, agreed he—(if
It squared with therapeutic protocol,—
Which it did almost always)—so I'd riff
On theories and conundrums;—but since he
Was never free for more than minutes five,—
My deeper myst'ries gyred within me.
To have a list'ning love's to be alive!—
And vuln'rable. For hours, you're all ears:—
Accepting you're!—but fear I outing fears.

Sonnet 75

Imagine, love, a skein of yarn:—perhaps
It's mustard yellow. Sadly, it's so tangled,
To pull on any end or loop entraps
It further. If, methodic'ly, you wrangled
With it all ev'ning, you, by slow degree,
Might loosen and rewrap it neatly into
A ball and make it useable by me
In my next afghan. Nat'rally, continue
To make such pretty, comforting home gifts
I'd love to—must, to tell the truth—do, even
If they're in mustard yellow:—though it lifts
My spirits, not all readily perceive in
The hue the loveliness I do. Oh bless you,
If my forsaken, loopy mind you'll rescue!

Sonnet 76

Hey chatterbox! Sit here, by me. Now, listen—
(Yes, close your lips!)—to this Tale of Tormentors
Who fled my brain—(for once)—upon—(some kissin',
Alright, dear, we'll do next!)—me finding renters
To share my house and also mortgage payment;—
Receiving lab results all negative;—
And seeking and destroying several latent,
False fears though "uncondition'l positive
Regard and empathy"—the trappings of
Rogerian, or person-centered, theory—
Which my new psychother—But, hello, love!—
You're of this Classic Yarn already weary?
Ah, kiss me then!—or else resume your chatter:—
When good I feel, details don't seem to matter!

Sonnet 77

My green eyes saw you:—me away you blew!
How cool and silv'ry,—warm and hot thou art!
Of all the hues, your favorite's turquoise blue!
Your gallery shows vibrant modern art!
The artists paint mixed media and canvas!
I'm tickled pink our stars decreed we'd meet!
Blank slated, I decided men to canvass!
We both like veggies colorful,—red meat!
I blush to note again your constant yack!
You look so fine in sky-blue shirt and jeans!
Your coat was knit from hunter wool of yak!
Your DNA must have some peachy genes!
Encode they beau-blue eyes and handed left!
This purple poem's done?—yep, nothin' left!

Sonnet 78

I dreamt your absence of, these last two nights:—
As cruelties rent dark rooms,—mix-ups got worse,
I knew you elsewhere were—by your own rights—
And soon, we wouldn't meet, write or converse.
This was just fact:—I neither ached nor moaned.
My grueling dreams, it's easy to perceive, were
Resemblances of real life:—you'd postponed
Our seventh date 'cause of a cough and fever.
This morning, Saturday—I'd hoping ceased
To see you—my three hens and I did wake
To see cicadas, hundreds:—what a feast!
Can I a feast of chicken soup you take?—
Not made of bugs or *my* birds, 'course! I'd, baby,
Your virus gladly catch!—I mean, um, . . . maybe.

Sonnet 79

Her neck is twisted toward us. Slender, pink-
Nailed fingers clasp her hip. Chicly appareled,
She holds her 20's stole around her—(mink?)—
Pale shoulders bared. (Is she Zelda Fitzgerald?)
Her coyness—(frisky eyes,—rouge-lipsticked smile,—
Chin lofty)—catches us off guard. Her ring's
A giant silver bauble—to beguile
Us till we're seized by golden glimmerings
In her lush headband, taming her thick bob.
Her string of pearls—(those any girl would covet)—
Loop wrongly down—(she's making our hearts throb)—
Her sloping back:—might she expose more of it?!
This painting you adore especially;—
Think you—by chance, heart—she's at all like me?

Sonnet 80

Jon Krakauer climbed up Mount Everest
And down again;—but not as lucky were
Some others on that day. He wrote, distressed,
The presence of a journalist could spur—
Perhaps—a mountaineer to push too hard:—
Most people fear in print to see themselves.
Did Ford, some forty years later, regard
His trysts with Carrie Fischer fit for shelves
At Barnes & Noble?—no, he threatened suing.
My—(now ex-)—in-law secrets heard me share:—
She wrote a scathing blog post!—I'm still stewing.
I name not you—nor E—yet true scenes bare;—
Is that alright? (Was Shakespeare more discreet?)
My plea:—I aim to honor, not mistreat. . . .

Sonnet 81

I sought to snag some virile, dreamboat dude
With long appendages:—your fingers wrap
And play chords easily, 'cause they extrude;—
Another part—let's just say—leaves no gap.
I sought to date some dext'rous DIYer:—
You built me wooden stands, were not aghast
To contemplate installing track-light wire
And, when you broke my backdrop,—fixed it fast.
I sought to charm some sportsman—(you play hockey)—
With intellect and street smarts—(you've got depth)—
A leader—(you da boss)—who isn't cocky;—
Your manliness, though, goes one further step:—
I never dreamed—not in my grandest wishes—
You'd be so macho. *Swoons*. (You washed my dishes?!)

Sonnet 82

I knew your body long before I knew you,—
And still I know you not so very much.
It's easier to teach than be a guru;—
It's harder to swap secrets than to touch.
In younger, college years, we had the time
And opportunities to form close bonds;—
But, as full-fledged adults, it feels sublime
When, in a day or two, your love responds.
Not having heard "I love you" in my childhood,
I've never understood how that phrase works.
Not soon those words say genuinely I could
'Cause them I'd loathe to bandy like knee jerks.
Yet, I—in bed—burst, "I adore you!" You—
Surprising me—chimed, "I adore you, too."

Sonnet 83

Without permission from authority!—
Audaciously!—I chopped in half my pills.
Their side effects minute are—I agree—
But still productive of too many ills.
I had all life essentials—(I could eat,
Shag you and sleep)—but when I strove to act—
(Run, garden, cook or clean)—I lay there beat,—
For energy to leave the couch I lacked.
Now that the dose is lesser, I can go
'Bout my pursuits alertly,—in a hurry;—
And life is vivid—(nature!—music!—woe!)—
Which can be sweet—or rough. A further worry:—
When potent molecules stay blocked in pill—
And don't me quell,—will you adore me still?

Sonnet 84

Two first-rate agents, both at once, requested
To read my manuscript. I would rejoice—
Except that—one—my novel I invested
With syntax recondite, a triple voice
And oddness and poetics people may
Balk at—if they are less than open to
Wild rounds of literary sport. (Now, gray
Sweetheart, please listen here—and me issue
Your thoughts.) I—two—obliged to news unveil,
Emailed a note:—real blunt!—no tact!—all biz!
Ah, shit. And yet,—she evals books, not mail;—
Think you I parse this right? Moreover, is
It possible to be too brusquely gritty—
When messaging a gal in New York City?

Sonnet 85

Sweet yack, you were, in our relationship—
(Before you'd said it all!)—the one who talks;—
When comfortable, I inhibition strip:—
Now I'm the—(how'd this happen?)—chatterbox!
We used to meet at my digs, bare and clean,—
Since in your own lived your ex-counterpart;—
We meet at yours now, empty and pristine:—
As tenants filled my home,—yours broke apart.
Heeled sandals gave me blisters,—curbed my movement,
So mannishly I'll style new ambulation;—
You taught me lots 'bout hockey, home improvement,
Grunge, fatherhood and—now—exfoliation!
We keep on flip-flopping our routine ways:—
That's cool!—so long as faithful passion stays.

Sonnet 86

Informed you me—on our date three—you're selfish.
I wasn't, though, alarmed. You meant, to own
A biz that pays takes perseverance. Hellish
You'd feel if your dream faded unbeknown.
Most people slave to meet austere demands
Imposed by friends, foes, fam'ly, beaus and strangers;—
But I'm with you:—I'd rather thrust my hands
Into that soil of fertileness and dangers
Where grows—robust or stunted—my ambition.
Instead of cringing in the status quo,
I wrote a book. I asked no fool permission
To postulate—some fifteen years ago—
I art and publication could achieve.
(Don't ever cease to listen,—hope,—believe.)

Sonnet 87

Love,—hear my cursed 'n' miserable lament!
My queries?—I've, by—(nearly)—everyone!—
Been slighted or ignored,—'spite what I sent.
This sonnet sequence?—too much is undone.
My day job?—boring, pointless and soul sucking.
My garden?—choked with weeds and vegetables
I've no arm strength to pick. You?—I'm not fucking
Right here and now:—life's not all :)s and LOLs!
My toenail polish?—smudged on some unknown
Home furnishing,—left—(where?)—a pinkish stain.
My budget, smart and new?—week one got blown.
"Wow. But what caused," you ask, "this streak of bane?"
Rash gods!—bad luck!—rude saps!—or is it—(grr)—
Just PMS? ("Yep!" winks the calendar.)

Sonnet 88

Your dream chick?—self-sufficient,—self-reliant!
She hustles no external validations:—
You'd lasso flappers—piquant and defiant—
Who bypass tourist roundups;—beach vacations;—
Consumerism;—body worshiping;—
And flat, discordant vibes—in favor of
Smarts;—confidence;—tuned purpose;—and a mien
Of optimistic concord,—fearless love.
You've—(silver fox!)—a thing for necks,—long hair,—
B cups,—smart classiness that's reminiscent
Of jazz and country,—understated flair,—
Wide, can-do smiles,—short skirts,—and headbands. Isn't
This wild:—I'm changed!—blue riffs of contradictions!—
Yet these—(cowboy!)—of me?—bull's-eye descriptions.

Sonnet 89

A stranger typed, "I'm F's mom. Shall we meet?"
Enthused I, "July 4?—let's ask your son!"
You said, "Let's you and me, alone, go—sweet!—
See fireworks;—now, wouldn't that be fun?"
Said I, "This book I'll buy that middle schooler,—
And, love, let's take him to a Shakespeare play!"
Replied you, "Nah, he other stuff finds cooler;—
To *Tempest* take him I'll myself one day."
Your dad, on hearing I've a homestead garden,
Bought me a big rain barrel;—I can't thank him,
Except through you. Your sisters, in posh jargon,
Typed jokes about your pic:—they seem so swank! Them
All meet I'd gladly. Yet, *his* comfort's prime;—
And wisdom whispers, "All in its own time."

Sonnet 90

The high, in Fahrenheit, in summer—(hottie!)—
Exceeds, most days, the number of this sonnet.
The hen, to cool her feather-mantled body,
Will spread her wings a little, whereupon it
Will seem she's too uncomfortable to be
Herself:—no scratching, gabbling or walking.
I brought my dears some milk with ice. The three
Sipped gratefully . . . then spilled it, flapping!—squawking!
This was my fault, not theirs. They knew no better,—
And neither does the stem of my emotions.
Like hens, my demons instinct, to the letter,
Obey,—without regard to sounder notions.
Stud,—we're in luck:—when hot, I still can guide!—
So I can stay the cool chick at your side.

Sonnet 91

When those Three Fates have spun a bad or good
Outcome,—at least I know just where I stand;—
To manage harder it's, at times, when "Could—
With luck—occur!" is all that can be planned.
One agency rejected me:—"Your writing
Is strong and smart." Aw, thanks!—but, now, who cares?
One needs more time:—for luck I'm jumpy,—fighting;—
It's like a game of musical "pub" chairs.
F, as you know, E ditched me,—this despite
Caresses, hugs and smiles,—which now mean zip.
"I'm not so sure," you gulped;—luck I'll indict—
(Alone!)—if you my fam'ly shindig skip.
And yet,—although—heart—treasures sway—in flux,—
Purrs wisdom, "Patience . . ."—Man, screw that! This sucks.

Sonnet 92

I dreamed of my P.T. last night:—again
Your presence therein was your absence, fox;—
And though I'd rather vision you, not him,—
The content of last night's trance . . . kinda rocks!
My ex-flame changed his mind,—badly desired
Me;—'cause of you, I had to him deflate
So said, "I have a boyfriend. I was fired
Up once, but now?—the spark's out. You're too late!"
This fantasy subliminal I relish
Not just for reasons obvious and trite—
(It's basely fun to make an ember jealous)—
But, too, I worry you don't me ignite
As E does—(did?!)—yet—candid babe—I gauge,
Though we're unsure, we're both here:—on this page.

Sonnet 93

So, we're both gun-shy?—ah, we've prudent sense.
Our last decisions blasted us down trails
To brambly holes. To perch, calm, on a fence
Seems wiser than to risk more thorny fails.
Besides, this rail's so peaceful;—you're here, too.
Why gambol off to clash with relatives,—
Where tastes are dubious, esteem's past due
And each debate its usefulness outlives?
Instead, I'll churn—(in print and vocal sound)—
Out compliments—(hey sexy!)—as you bring
Your tools up here,—fix all that's me around:—
We're lovebirds 'fraid to fly,—though not to sing.
Desire we only what we've long-time had;—
Then, why do—picket-mate—I feel so bad?

Sonnet 94

Are curious you 'bout my former beaus?
Guys slip into a gal's life and—they say—
Soon slip out,—while her girlfriend count just grows.
Well, A was artsy, smart and—turns out—gay.
Then, B was quiet,—timid:—not my type.
Cool hair had C,—but just my bod he wanted.
To dump D's scorn the time was overripe.
My escapades with E I've spilled and vaunted.
Now, forthright F:—you're not another slipup!
There's not a lesser man behind the curtain!
No way you're just a 'specia'ly tasty hiccup!
And "they" don't—I'm unquestionably certain—
Know jack!—or us. To do with *that* we've much.
We clearly—(*right?*)—will stay in—lovey—touch.

Sonnet 95

"Woolf, Lincoln, Melville, Kafka, King and Poe—
Were all misjudged and blocked!—yet, when extinct,
Got praise and love," I gushed. My mom gasped, "Oh:—
Like Trump!" *Our wavelengths aren't, exactly, synced.*
I heard my girlfriends talking. "So, I told
My boyfriend—ha ha, faulty is his brain—
To buy me fresher flowers,—pricey gold!"
"I'm training my man, too." *Are they insane?*
That agent—hope she'd given me—wrote, "With
It simply we did not connect." *I'm sunk.*
You smiled, us ordered beer and said, "A myth—
That 'merica's not great. Greed's so much bunk.
Entice 'em with a new book." Yuenglings clinking,
I grinned right back. *That's just what I was thinking!*

Sonnet 96

I won't forget my both-arms injured years,—
When struggled I to hold a fork or book up,
Swing arms to run, dress, type and drive. The gears
Of my submind, moreover, got so shook up,
I woke from every sleep with muscle tension
In jaw,—arms,—butt,—legs,—feet. I was twice broken:—
Rep. strain,—then night's inflame. I slow ascension
Had only 'cause my body stayed outspoken:—
Pain's good!—a nat'ral stop sign, indicating,
"K., that's enough." The hard part is to listen—
And warnings heed. Too, signs pop up in dating:—
When do I feel more angst, with him?—or missin'?
Here's how I know you're not just misused ink:—
When you're nearby,—I don't feel drove to drink!

Sonnet 97

What type of woman do you want to date?
What do you mean, you are not sure? Before
Commencing dating, didn't formulate
You notions on what traits you could adore?
You haven't heard the maxim 'bout the road
That won't direct you to delightful places
If fierce initiative you never showed
When took you your initial, eager paces?
We both have reservations 'bout you-me;—
But mine are due to yours:—I fall in love
When cherished. I had this epiphany:—
Aside E's force, perhaps, you need to shove!
With whom do I wish—cozily—to nestle?—
A man like you . . . who also thinks I'm special.

Sonnet 98

Now—white or black knight—twenty times we've dated.
From my move one, this strategy I've charted:—
Me plus entrepreneur. Yet, this checkmated
My checked-out side as I'd just—(barely!)—started
To make my moves. While independence is
The hallmark attribute of what I want,
The true self-starter needs no help:—just his
One piece;—I've thus been captured *en passant*!
Arrested you my effort to leap forward,
Although the game was young. An upstart pawn,
I'm lifted up by what your fingers ordered!—
Then put down,—sidelined,—taken,—useless:—gone.
Sweet, sovereign king!—of course you castled free.
My consolation prize?—the queen's mighty. . . .

Sonnet 99

If you, bright lamp, were flickering toward trouble,
I'd surge to save you. But,—you're self-sustaining.
Well, so am I! Despite—and 'midst—the rubble
Of my morale,—shall I resume web dating?
A week ago, we broke. Now dimmed the sun
Has, though it's 3 p.m. Eclipse my brightness
No moon—or man—for long can. "Having fun—"
You shed a light, "—we were. What sex!" You're right, yes.
Yet, sunshine,—had we more?—a whiter prong?
My demons shrieked, "He's not that into you!"
Hot, heav'nly body:—they, for once, weren't wrong;—
Even the crassest tabloids can speak true.
I'll shine!—be lucid stone!—lest darkened I'm
By pleasures fitting slickly . . .—O nighttime!

Sonnet 100

My bar was low, dear F, because of E;—
How could another man ever attain
Those peaks of caregiving virility:—
To be, at once, so manly and humane?
Impossible for this to twice transpire,—
And so I chose to settle for great sex;—
Achieved this fully I! Babe, I admire
Your earthy, potent feel!—but what connects
A couple of joy-diggers thrust together,—
When one's unsure,—the other pines for skies?
I have immense respect for regions nether:—
Don't get me wrong. We'd selfish be and wise
To romp in muck—(if safe!)—quite frequently,—
While bravely mounting toward sublimity.

Sonnet 101

I see now—stud—we've jostled down into
The sunken ruts of past, failed partnerships:—
Resumed I taking mindlessly my cue
From every frothy clue spit from your lips,—
On you relying for all self-regard—
(An endless quest for warrant to be me)—
As you withdrew affection,—turning hard,
Aloof and cold as can a stallion be.
When I feel underloved—(for me, not rare)—
My instinct is to love—and show it—more,—
As if the heartfelt feelings of a mare
Replenish could of love the worldly store.
I lost my reigns;—and rutting lost its charm.
If I reset my wheels,—that'd do no harm.

Sonnet 102

Lost, darling, blue-eyed doll:—perceived I signs
Of tumult as we gorged on steamy summer,—
Yet them ignored. For one—you'd vague designs
To flee the state,—yet never said a bummer
It'd be to leave me. Two—you showered moi
With help and yack—but parched with scanty praise.
And when I tossed you—this is number trois—
Confettied language—(sweet, warm sobriquets,—
Endearments,—accolades)—you sat unmoved.
Let's—Sagitt—to astrology surrender:—
You're independent,—venturesome—(wow, proved
Are stars?)—but tactless,—flighty,—rarely tender;—
I'm delicate,—too trusting. Breach would happen,—
'Cause:—constellations! (I believe that crap, then?)

Sonnet 103

O handsome!—can I call you that once more?
You s'pposed my nothings sweet weren't fully truthful,—
But what's not lovely 'bout you? I adore
Your spunky strength,—cute nose 'n' spirit youthful,—
Ash hair 'n' outlook wise. I read a book
That changed my life. It said, one must be brave.
Yourself throw out there honestly. If shook
Up by a fall, stand up,—your failure waive
Off as experience,—what went astray
Assess,—fix errors,—don't lose hope,—anew
Give what's you genuinely. (Thanks, Brené!)
I do this with my novel,—now, with you.
I write:—rejection is my cross. It's—thus—
Gratuitous when you're "not right for" us!

Sonnet 104

The irony! While injured and on leave
From work, required I expensive tech
And costly therapies that might relieve
My symptoms, bod and brain:—a duple wreck;—
I'd no cash flow. The irony! My phone
Had rad voice recognition software;—I
Used fingers, 'cause 'bout this I hadn't known:—
Technology's intent's to simplify,—
Yet's too complex. The irony! To be
Controller of her bod, a woman's righted;—
The pill her anxious makes. The irony!
My one pure love for E flared unrequited,—
So strived I to extinguish it through you;—
Dang!—now I've true loves unrequited two.

Sonnet 105

Inquisitive, I wonder! What is it
About you twain that love's glow me provides?
Is it 'cause on your sep'rate thrones you sit:—
The expert pros,—the gentle, honest guides?
And what's the best technique for anti-stoking
My two-tongued flame for sals superbly smiley,
Suave, subtle, sound of character and smoking
Hot? How'm I s'possed to live—(I must unshyly
Inquire, good gentlemen)—without recourse
To—(one's enough, though!)—finely formed, full phalli,—
Since I've no zest for walk-of-shame remorse?
But my most pressing question—ask it shall I?—
Is, what am I supposed to do—(dish dears!)—
With all this extra gin and Yuengling beers?

Sonnet 106

You were my bling-bling stars,—my twinklin' swag:—
I miss your shooter weakness,—pricks sustained;—
A telescope I'd mount, high on a crag—
If lenses their phenomena retrained.
Although you've faded from my naked eye—
Twin aughts to all who crane their necks out back—
You still, like Martians flying—rarely—by,
Sporadic waves beam through the zodiac.
Clear nights, I sometimes my desires distort,—
Articulate a query apropos
Of art—or arms;—dim glimmers soon report:—
My staticky, Platonic radio.
Gray Castor:—that we write as friends I'm cheered!
Immortal Pollux:—please stop acting weird. . . .

Sonnet 107

'Bout-face. Backtrack. Debug. Recalibrate.
She's baaack!! I broadcast to that sausage fest
On that ol' website:—nope, it's not too late!
If asswipes wanna ping me?—be my guest!
See, this time, playing I'm a diff'rent game.
Ingenious Gemini, your high jinks tricked
Me twice:—if I'm the hunter, I'm to blame
For catching only junk. I'll prey constrict
Myself to being,—arrows wait here for:—
Unmotivated dudes I won't, then, meet—
But only those out mauling my front door—
Or—these I'll answer—tapping nice 'n' sweet.
Twins,—do you care?—an eye doc on I led—
And dropped! Up next?—a physicist-and-fed. . . .

Sonnet 108

High, double stars:—I'm grounded,—down here weary,
Confused and trampled. Dreamt I total power
You, E, had o'er a harem. Guilt-wracked, teary,—
You pledged to be more ethical. A shower
I took. You word sent on which earrings wear
I should. I—longing for you—nursed an achy
Euphoria:—it nice felt!—not, though, fair.
F, just day visions—(was our bond that flaky?)—
You haunt:—blasé, you chew your gum. Obv'ously,
Your, E, strong rope 'round me is twisted. Do,
F, pine for me you ever in non-lusty,
Admiring, caring ways? E, how 'bout you?
Important:—you were simply rebound flings!
I must now nurture, guard and use my wings.

Sonnet 109

By night I weigh up one of you;—by day
The other. Saintly yin:—your secrets cache
You in your hair-shirt cage. Lay yang:—you say
All freely, buoyantly and with panache.
Duality has likewise manifested
In twin first dates I went on recently:—
The ophthal, easygoing, drank 'n' jested;—
The fed, reserved, remained a mystery.
In sunshine, it's mad fun to laugh and frolic,—
Yet afterward, there's nothing left to ponder.
The depth and guts, though, of a melancholic
Indulge my blood's veiled lust to brood and wander.
Eye doc flies planes,—but I don't crave those highs.
I'll turn stone two:—this fed seems real—and wise.

Sonnet 110

I didn't lead that ophth on purposely!
Lost stars:—although I know not just myself
But also which male types I'd like to see,
I can't just line up traits upon a shelf—
As if they're specimens all codified—
But need to test my theories in real life,—
Say, gauging how it feels to be allied
To one with faith—(too much internal strife)—
Or without kids—(to help some I'm inclined)—
Yet,—all my first instincts panned out correct!
My friends say I should take some time to find
Myself:—form tastes,—amend every defect.
I'm found, though!—why impose a no-sex blight?
Too, in that case,—about what would I write?

Sonnet 111

My friends—in their considerable wisdom—
(I say this not in sarcasm;—they're savvy)—
Claim this:—the grown male hominid has his thumb
Upon the scales. He is the choosing half,—she,
In contrast, the receiver of esteem.
The hot pursuit, initially, that guys
Engage in makes gals' passions more than dream:—
Men what they want do;—women compromise.
This my pathetic love installments show:—
No matter how acute my pain, my plea
Would only make more resolute your no.
I'm sick of play'n' the fool:—let them woo me!
Does this game plan make me a jaded churl,—
Or is it just smart dating, as a girl?

Sonnet 112

All seemed so promising—yet low turned out.
My second date—and last—with said fed agent
Revealed my trusty instincts aren't without
Their faults. The cosmic mystery that latent—
Or so I thought—hid in this man dissolved
Like chemical reagents in some dirty,
Sad, dungeon lab'ratory. I evolved,
In college, from a science major nerdy
To what I'm now:—a diff'rent kind of seeker;—
My mom and dad would love a STEM dude as
A son-in-law—NO! He can take his beaker—
Said stealthy fed—and *poof!* Plus, whew!—whereas
You dress my poems—(thank you, twin heartthrob!)—
I shan't lay bare his veiled, top-secret job!

Sonnet 113

Y' know, dreamboats?—I had the perfect tack
All 'long. But when you tossed me overboard,
I left all confidence in my wake's track
Upon your decks,—assumed I had ignored
Some basic truths on how to tie a knot:—
But, 'course, it's possible to navigate
Superbly,—trimly rig the world's best yacht—
And still obtain chilled drowning as one's fate.
An "act of gods" it was that smacked wet salt
'Pon my lone mouth, 'stead of your pirates' lips.
My friends, ashore, make maps;—they're not at fault
If I've a better view, out on these ships:—
Barge, ironclad, sloop, schooner or canoe?—
From now on, *I'll* decide which to *pursue*!

Sonnet 114

All's fair in love—but only if she's strong!
I don't see how a tamped-down, passive me
Could lead to mutual respect;—it's wrong
And, frankly, gross to weave a tapestry
Of weft without a warp—or vice versa,—
Then try to use those loose and sep'rate threads
To warm a couple's nights. The media,
For centuries, have told us that our beds
Should be enwrapped in thick, huge, manly cords
That pin her, so all she can do is glance—
In silent awe—at what true love affords
When mates equality swap for romance.
Where's he who'll weave—(if not you, absent strands)—
With tension matching mine,—with humble hands?

Sonnet 115

My dear loose ends:—to clarify my stance,
I don't think men and women are the same;—
While culture dictates part of circumstance,
Our genomes, too, locked down who we became.
You watch'n' play team sports and care who won;—
Most everything inside my purse is pink;—
I think clothes shopping is bedazz'lin' fun;—
You're great at spurring moving parts to sync.
What's due to culture, what to pers'nal quirks
And what to sex type? All I know's when we
Pursue each other ardently,—that works!—
Though we do go about things diff'rently.
You boys seek sex and love;—we girls—I fear—
Seek love and sex. (Wait,—what's the problem here?)

Sonnet 116

It's been a month since I have gotten laid,—
Which brings me down:—it's just biology.
You, former P.T., can't, you've shown, be swayed,—
But, artsy biz pro, you'll, with luck, agree.
Before I act:—is "friends with benefits"
A prudent tactic? Should she sex refuse
Him, so to bribe his love? If she permits,
Will access lure him closer? Which sad ruse
Is craftier?—wiser? My girlfriends cried,
"Preserve your treasure!" "That's bullshit. Indulge,"
A straight guy counseled me. "You'll have him tied!"
Too late:—my mind's made up. My girls divulge,
A vibrator's a winsome substitution;—
I favor, though, the all-nat'ral solution!

Sonnet 117

F:—(this one's all for you!)—my boy-toy plaything
I thought you'd be. We'd halt the sexless drudge—
(For safety, exclusivity maintaining)—
Till transcendent'ler loves moved us to budge.
But early, beautiful, free bird!—you showed
An hour 'fore the time we had arranged;—
You, chatting as I cooked, eagerly glowed;—
In bed, our amorousness hadn't changed.
If we exclusively make love, admire,
Adore and miss,—is that so diff'rent than
A boyfriend-girlfriend nesting? Why so dire
Is—dinosaur!—your thirst for a wingspan
That, fully spread, extends from cave to sea?
Well, sweet!—such openness helps me be me.

Sonnet 118

As you're my muse—winged one—so I've, it seems,
Inspired you in turn. Your verses shimmer
With heartfelt, sweet, expressive, nimble gleams
Of unpretentious truth. Our weeks-long simmer
Of passion, flaring low as we compared
Us to fell slews of lesser matches, cured
Our meat:—we raised our swords, high as we dared!—
And slayed our loving beast. Her greed we've heard!—
And heeded. I've your heart! . . . no more. Is this
The poem that will win your head? Fonder
I'm of your rhymes than Shakes' exquisite bliss!—
Though you they may not win the Pulitzer.
Will you accept a less than perfect 10?
Birdbrain!—how mighty, really, is the pen?

Sonnet 119

Since I'm good-hearted, I'll do you this favor:—
You're still unsure—(poor dear)—so here are lists
Of pros and cons, to help you cease to waver
And confident feel 'bout your future trysts.
The pros:—you missed me, these five lonely weeks;—
You claim no sweetheart's praised you as I do;—
My grace and beauty are, you wrote, mystiques
Corporeal and of the spirit, too;—
We sync—(we're rare)—on every last issue;—
Your life, you said, improved after we met;—
I cried, "Am I not blond enough for you?"
To which you yelped, "I'm glad you're a brunette!"
The con:—you might a better woman find.
Let's see,—which list is longer, when aligned?

Sonnet 120

It's been twelve months since sonnets I began
To write. Now autumn's come again. You flew—
A scrawny, headstrong, innocent, young man—
Down Under, suddenly!—though you'd no clue
What to expect. Just like that plucky teen
You were,—I also took a yearlong trip;—
I journeyed far into the unforeseen:—
Without abandoning my homestead ship.
Now off the meds and feeling A-OK,
I'm piloting my love life,—showing me.
When folks their artwork wish to frame, you say
It's best to snap-decide—and not to be
Irresolute;—they're both real nice. Just choose
The rustic, brown one:—lark, you've zip to lose!

Sonnet 121

The gullible female between eighteen
And sixty-five has instant recourse to
The plentitudes of web and magazine
Sagacities:—*He's Really Into You . . .*
Or Is He? screams a headline;—but, alas,
As I'm not in that demographic group,
I'll add my own bullshit to my own sass
And me advise if I should bawl or whoop:
If "Did you, L, on dates, think just of me?"
"Are you composing poems for me still?"
"Don't worry!" and "One-woman man!" cries he,
Then—(rosy findings, heart, I shall distill!)—
He's into you,—just doesn't know it yet.
Next up:—*Is Your Intelligence a Threat?*

Sonnet 122

Your body's signage shows you're hankering
To talk with,—lay eyes on,—make love to me;—
But, patient and polite, you wait for green—
And only then the gas hit joyously.
The billboards of your soul announce in tall,
Prismatic letters that our traffic needs
To take it slow:—all crossroads at a crawl;—
Abruptly, though, you'll shift to higher speeds.
You say, since you're too scatterbrained to drive
Through multiple gals' signals, left and right,—
You'll zoom:—till you at love's red disk arrive.
Since I can't say who's—(yellowed you've my light)—
Hot-rodding toward your biz—with flashy eyes,—
Reluctantly, I'm chasing other guys.

Sonnet 123

What smell you in the glass, dear boy? I'm lost.
Tonight we meet again;—but, meanwhile, we've
Both dating profiles full of dregs we've crossed
Off of our lists,—while scheming we're to thieve
A winner from the competition's bar:—
A choicer one, that is, than you or me.
The used bookstore's, likewise, a reservoir
Of dull, picked-over pulp:—the matchless prix
Is in the new batch, just arrived!—and yet
Folks often overlook a dark horse wine,—
So I'll scan closely, taste and place my bet.
I'd rather blend my grapes with your bloodline!—
I think:—my taste buds can be hard to read.
My course?—I'll sip! . . . unless you intercede.

Sonnet 124

I once, naive, let others choose for me;—
Now I'm directing my own classic flick:—
I climbed your steps, picked my philosophy—
And hoped that sovereignty would do the trick.
Since this one—costar—ain't no horror film,
I checked my head was screwed on super tight:—
I'm yours, I'd hint, but only if you will
Be mine;—if not, let's just get laid tonight.
This was a documentary, I thought,
In which a tough gal tries to catch a fish
But, boringly, is never wholly caught,—
Till softened you the light—all dramaish!—
And sang, "I'm taking down my profiles, k?"
I—spotlit, doelike—had no lines to say!

Sonnet 125

So came an awkward pause. I sat up,—turned
To peer in your blue crescent eyes, surprised:—
I'd spun my plotline so to not get burned—
And couldn't easily be hypnotized.
I saw, though, you were serious and meant,
Again we'd partners be—resume our journey—
But 'stead of pitching you a soft assent,
I cried, "I've messaging been this attorney!"
"D'you wanna—" spoke you candidly, "—keep writing?
We—sweet—aren't wedding,—moving in,—just dating:—
I've tossed my qualms 'bout be'ng with you. Exciting
It'd be to bring—but bleak and suffocating—
An 'Angel' to art shows;—I favor you!"
You haven't heard 'bout my V.S. debut?!

Sonnet 126

Okay,—I'm not a model;—though my wings
Might pretty be, they're also wry, verbose
And tending toward audacity and stings,—
Especia'ly when a playmate gets too close.
The myth of Icarus reveals that flight
Is not at fault if one gets burnt or wet,
Since aviators can control their height
'Tween sun and sea,—keep excesses unmet.
This balance, then, I'll strive for as I soar:—
To love you while remaining solely me;—
To be content but also work for more;—
To fly together with you, sep'rately.
To be your wiseass bunny I aspire:—
My profile, playboy?—all set to expire!

Sonnet 127

Sweet, handsome man:—this feels precarious!
While dating 'round, I'd think, if one's a dud—
(Lacks sex appeal—or ditches me)—no fuss
I'd make—but simply snatch a diff'rent stud.
More fraught is my relationship with you:—
I call you, 'gain, my boyfriend—ah, so nice—
My hard-won liberty, though, might unscrew,—
And how I'd suffer if you dumped me twice!
Last time around, you flipped when I spoke of
Fam'ly soirees,—so this time circumspect
I'm with all jeopardous discourse;—I love
You, though:—oh, this I longed to interject
Into our bedroom fusion! I held back;—
And now I'm tipping, gagged and maniac. . . .

Sonnet 128

I like that what you make is solid,—real.
You paint a rowboat scene,—refinish tables,—
Construct a deck:—all tangible. From zeal
And guts you built a business;—it enables
The art community to sell their work:—
Now all can see the vibrant, mod result.
From fatherhood you also do not shirk;—
You're slowly nurt'ring child into adult.
Me, though?—I harvest vegetables and fruits,
Raise hens for eggs, cook healthy food and run:—
All bodily! Yet, *these* quixotic roots—
My writings—are elusive:—see no sun.
Long, toilsome years make only bytes in cloud;—
Touch me:—you're so substantially endowed!

Sonnet 129

Some couples flip off lamps and candles light
To dial the ambiance more luscious,—hotter;—
Some switch the furnace off and build, at night,
A charming fire;—we shut off the water!
Babe, nothing sets the mood like four or five
Trips to the hardware store because the first,
Second and third times home we did arrive,
Some part forgot we for this job accursed!
And nothing says romance like full-on panic:—
Like knowing, since you fucked up, it befalls,
We can't cook, wash or flush tonight—mechanic—
Or watching rivers gush down through the walls!
I'm so glad we tooled back for one last screw;—
My shower's fixed:—I need it,—after you!

Sonnet 130

My girlfriends photos post of them abroad;—
Guys' profiles often say they love to travel;—
But me?—I'd rather leave the globe untrod,
Since fleeing home makes everything unravel:—
While gone, I worry 'bout my chickens' health
And garden's keep in someone else's care,—
A migraine get,—lament the loss of wealth,—
And, 'cause I can't work out or write, despair!
Although your web profile made zero mention
Of this polemic issue—(cuckoo!)—(loon!)—
Let slip you your, till now, concealed intention:—
"We'll journey 'round the world together soon!"
"Wha-what?!" I gasped—and made a fast egress;—
I need to pack some bags:—the answer's yes!

Sonnet 131

But first,—I need to tell you some key stuff.
I have internal conflict:—hushed I'm, lest
You startle,—fly off;—yet I've had enough
Of hiding my brash self,—afraid,—repressed.
The last time that I cowered, caved and cried
To please a stubborn man, I saw the brink,—
My muscles trashed and psyche tanked. I lied,
See, baby blue:—boy, that's some toxic drink.
If I share honest feelings, strange and nutty
Plans, brazen hopes and offbeat views,—yet grieve
You my distinctive selfhood, I'll feel smutty;—
But this I have to risk:—take me—or leave.
I zipped your lips, explained this and you told,
"I love you."—yikes! I'm edgy!—open!—bold!

Sonnet 132

Unzipping you's the easy part! You, smiley,
Were nodding in concordance, as I spouted;—
Once freed to vocalize, you praised me highly
For not concealing who I am. You'd doubted
My rightness for you, you explained, because
It's hard to find one's lighted-perfect shot
Amidst the flash of others' tricked cam'ras,—
The pageantry of all that you've been taught.
Your wish?—to be that skilled photographer
Whose eagle eye can spot the homely girl
Who, through your lens, shines chicer,—comelier
Than all the rest:—your found, clandestine pearl.
Then:—when, from secrecy, I came to light,—
To take you there, too,—you did me invite!

Sonnet 133

Some lady, in the cinema's bathroom,
Let run the faucet as she strolled away;—
My friend exclaimed, "How rude! Does she presume
That wasting water is, somehow, okay?"
Soon after, I, too, washed my hands and strode
Off from a gushing stream:—sinks automatic
We're all, see, used to. Subminds deeds encode—
And mindlessly repeat,—obtuse,—dogmatic.
Although my fam'ly taught that women can
Be leaders,—when I home left, I assumed
I couldn't cope without some certain man:—
To habits of submission I was doomed.
My luck:—the mind, with work, can artfully
Retrain;—now, hon, you say you'll follow me!

Sonnet 134

This is the poem I'm too good to write:—
Babe, sometimes my poetic subject sings,—
But this one, sadly, has a smarmy bite.
I'm angry with that fed—(our revelings
Consisted of two dates—and one long kiss)—
'Cause his emotions are so overblown,
He's 'shamed and fragile,—says I was remiss
In not informing him from you I'd flown
One week before:—as if a trigger warning
I need on me. I didn't for the hills
Run 'cause of you:—post-date and in the morning,
I felt stamped out. His low self-image kills
All joy;—and mine?—none of his biz. Heart, he's
To guilt-control me trying. Warning:—sleaze!!

Sonnet 135

You're diff'rent, prison break. Your attitude
Is that you strive to do outstanding work,
In personal and office life—both. You'd,
To lure in someone, never act the jerk:—
Manipulation ain't your style. You say,
The litmus for how good or bad you're doing
Is if your clients pleased are—and I stay;—
If not, you fix yourself,—not go 'round suing.
Folks say the bully's impetus is shame:—
They screen self-loathing under tough chainmail
And wield a knife to elsewhere lay the blame;—
Dear, that's one horribly unhealthy jail.
I've been locked up:—so lonely, that barred view!
Strange:—I'm content alone—thus can have you.

Sonnet 136

"You're full of shit. You make decisions poorly.
You suck at using words. Quit writing novels."
If such says one lean, crew-cut golf pro, sorely
He needs psych'therapy;—and if she grovels
And says he's right, she needs it, too. If twelve
Months after she has healed and that one left,
A long-haired physicist declaims, "Let's delve
Into my baggage. What,—now you've bereft
Me? But I overshared with you!" "Your fiction
Is great—phenomenal!—not that I've read it."
And "We had fun;—you fled:—that's contradiction!"
Then she should sprint the faster, not regret it,—
No matter how quaintly those gaslights shine.
Ah, thank you, heart:—you let me me define!

Sonnet 137

Alright,—I'm not so fragrant, either. Fawning
Susceptible I'm to:—I'll sweat to please,—
Eliciting back-scratches. Truth then dawning,
I'll seasons change—the day abruptly seize—
And gather all my rosebuds. Pierced, irate,—
My fawns'll claim my garden was all theirs!—
Though only me they'd worked to cultivate:—
In praise I hide,—till cashing in my shares.
I see now saccharine approval seeking
Can only bear the sun's harsh scrutiny
If grown in lush veracity;—no sneaking
'Midst alleyways allowed:—I must play me.
I'm skipping toward the blunter, open flowers:—
Like you! In love—not flattery—true power's.

Sonnet 138

I didn't mean to write about those guys;—
I don't desire revenge,—nor to malign:—
Aim only I to home discerning eyes,—
'Cause being nice?—another form of ly'ng.
A sage, angelic man my life has saved—
(Thank stars, sweetheart, you've not a jealous bone)—
And, for so long, to pay him back I craved;—
But, oh,—my presents ceased he to condone.
Then read I this:—if someone saves your life,
You save should someone else's, if you can;—
So many songs can play a lute and fife,—
But I've been vamping to the ol' cancan?!
I'm not a doctor, lifeguard, cop or shrink,—
Yet rescue someone could this candid ink?

Sonnet 139

One year ago, this week, I quit as E's
Trainee and patient. Soon, his bedfellow
I—briefly—was. Though I, like Socrates,
Could endlessly him pester, this I know:—
His influence on me was wholly good.
He helped me see I'm in-out beautiful;—
His bravos served to boost—not change—selfhood;—
We both were honest, kind and ethical.
I have a fantasy he'll call and say
A year he waited, 'cause some policy . . .—
What nonsense! His truth stumble on I may;—
More likely, po'ms 'bout him expose just me.
That man—not therapist—I don't know. You're,
Besides—sweet open book—my fave amour!

Sonnet 140

I've read you like a book of poems, dear:—
That is,—turns out I misinterpreted
So many of your feet, the biosphere
I surveyed, corralled, fed and shepherded
Into my sonnets isn't quite your ranch.
A free bird?—not so fast! You make li'l hops
From homey nest, to me, to your biz branch:—
Eschewing further, more exotic stops.
Since you're not clingy, flighty read my eyes:—
No bones!—I didn't take into account
You might duck both extremes. You yack, likewise,
Not wildly,—but just the perfect 'mount.
Is possible objective, true memoir?
I sure adore you:—whoever you are!

Sonnet 141

I don't know much about ice hockey, love,—
But, having witnessed sev'ral of your games,
I see the main objective is don't shove
A bruiser as you call him raunchy names—
But channel all your fury and frustration
Toward whaling on that puck haphazardly—
(A penalty comes from unchecked temptation,—
But slamming noises?—satisfactory!)—
The secondary goal being don't skate
At maximum, near-wipe-out speeds:—restrain
So not to—having stopped or turned too late—
Get dislocations,—broke bones,—throbbing pain.
I don't know much 'bout sports,—but it does seem,
You're—gentle lamb—the best man on your team!

Sonnet 142

My modus operandi's to support:—
I bundle up, show for your bod concern
And rah-rah as you play that icy sport,—
Not anything expecting in return.
You crushed, though, my self-melting paradigm—
When you encouraged me to join a pack
Of runners speeding through the wint'ry clime,
Six, eight, ten—and more—miles. I aback
Was taken:—if I race with that tough crowd,
You'll see me less. I felt, next, dumbstruck bliss:—
You said, to watch me finish you'd be proud.
A man who'll cheer me?—I'm not used to this!
Shocked I should not be to attain my share;—
But—(sports-'n'-me fan!)—what we have's too rare.

Sonnet 143

My chickens nonchalantly scratch for food
As sit I, on my back deck, hearing them.
As humans, you and I are kinda screwed,—
'Cause, unlike hens, we tend to us condemn.
So not to seem too eager, I might wait
Some 24 before you pinging. Next,
Will gradually my stomach ulcerate—
Each minute sense I no incoming text.
My chin is weak!—my jeans no longer fit!—
My face is blemished,—hair falls frizzily!—
You seemed cooled off last email! (You admit
You similar thoughts have;—it's not just me.)
I'm glad I'm meta:—not feathered,—joke-deaf.
My phone vibe-dings:—I jump! It says, Love, F.

Sonnet 144

Love:—fluster I, whilst I your billet-doux
Peruse;—this one you signed off, "Á bientôt!"
What means this lovely mot juste, writ by you?—
These words par excellence?—fuck if I know.
You—and the translators of Proust—and Tolstoy—
Seem not to get, I've studied German,—Spanish:—
That's it! When faced with beaux gestes,—I act most coy.
(The poseur's main faux pas?—she just ain't clannish.)
But my flagging esprit does swiftly rally!
(My joie de vivre's—baby—legendary!)
I shan't be long hors de combat:—I sally—
(With sangfroid, bébé)—through my dictionary. . . .
Voilá!—this sonnet's denouement is nigh!
Sheesh:—all that work, and all you said's "Good-bye"?

Sonnet 145

You've this commendable, uncommon talent:—
You with most anyone can get along.
Thus, you could date all kinds of women! Gallant
You were—(um, not)—to point this out. Not wrong
Were you, that long-gone day;—yet see exhibit
F:—two erotic-bodied lovers,—kissing
And throwing clothes with nothing to inhibit
Them from debating,—scheming,—reminiscing. . . .
O love,—how we can talk! Now watch how we,
Buck naked, try to pin some point of logic:—
As one of us gets urgently horny,—
The other introduces a new topic!
I hold, therefore, I'm 'specia'ly right for you;—
That's settled, then?—k., let's shut up 'n' screw!

Sonnet 146

Books are my passion. Yet—dear brainiac—
Mental acuteness often counters words:—
The wisest folk instinctively hijack
Old stories cherished by pedantic nerds.
Like you, I regularly work to quell
The messages 'bout dating people holler:—
Our culture wants to diamonds,—vacays sell;—
My loved ones wish 'pon me a bookish scholar.
They think a man, so to my soul beguile,
Must literary be. Ah, nope!—it warms
Imagining a non-bibliophile—
Who's not afraid to swerve out from the norms.
You seldom read,—yet practice higher art,—
Deciphering what stars wrote in your heart.

Sonnet 147

What girl—(li'l boy)—would hope for gold 'n' jewels—
When she could poetry recite aloud
As, int'rested, he listens?—when she drools,
And has for decades, for this scene? *I'm wowed!*
What gal—(tough guy)—would wish to dip her toes
In salty waves upon some island beach—
When she could run eight miles 'n' get half froze
As he, beside her, bikes? *I've lost my speech!*
What woman—(yummy man)—would want cocktails,
Each with a cute umbrella decoration,—
When she 'n' he could stir her homegrown kale's
Nutritiousness in pasta? *Whoa,—elation!*
Fulfilled you've all my foremost fantasies:—
Your turn! How can I—(gray young'un)—you please?

Sonnet 148

Last year, I hire'd—in secret—a divorce
Attorney;—*that same night*, my husband's ring
Pinched 'round his swelling, puffed finger with force,—
Though he knew zilch. (We stripped it with a string.)
It felt wrong, cashing in my wedding band;—
That ho-ur, I with an imam crashed cars.
To rush the funds to charity I'd planned—
And did—but quicker still were karmic stars?
I found you—(Starry "Knight")—in my *first* batch
Of matches. Now most days a sunny smile
You send:—with exclamation points!! Dispatch
The blues you never. ('Xcept after your trial.)
One-hundred percent true these stories are.
Yet will a soul believe? They're so bizarre. . . .

Sonnet 149

Aha!—see, I was right. You just admitted
You are a free bird—and a chatterbox!
The ground's not so root crazed—nor I dimwitted—
It'd throw me, this far off the starting blocks!
In physics class, I learned, events are flukes;—
Who can predict where particles will jump?
Lit deconstruction, learned I next, rebukes—
For thinking words mean stuff—the simple chump!
Since all possible outcomes could come true,—
And language can't communicate one thing,—
It's tempting to assume I can't construe
Your character, from it just witnessing.
But wait:—there's solid earth beneath my feet!
I'm drafting—as you fly, yack and repeat!

Sonnet 150

This is the time of year when we give thanks
And wolf down pie and turkey with the fam;—
This holiday, in my opinion, ranks
Among the best. We're going on the lam!—
But sep'rately. We'll both be shipping west:—
By air, I'll zoom off from your auto's flight;—
Not you, nor me, will be an awkward guest,—
And our relationship won't cling too tight.
While in the clouds, on mem'ries gray I'll feast:
The day your dad's rain barrel you reclaimed,
We reconciled. And this:—"When we're back east,
You want to meet my kiddo?" you exclaimed.
Love's pilgrim!—I'll pig out,—go back for more,—
Far more than bread and wine be grateful for.

Sonnet 151

Achilles and the tortoise:—who will win?
I used to think Achilles' feet would blaze
A burnt-out trail and finish first, braggin'!—
No matter what math tricks ol' Zeno plays.
But—(hero!)—how'd I overlook that heel?
Impatient, ardent, stubborn, flawed:—that's me;—
Swift-footed warriors no race can steal
When overtraining's led to injury.
The tortoise doesn't let impassioned pride
Incite her into nonstop composition;—
She'll hike 'mong "poetrees" till bleary eyed,
Then rest,—renewing muscles and cognition.
When harelike loved I,—I got burned!—and so
Let's—(demigod!)—be epic,—firm,—snug,—slow.

Sonnet 152

Your poem-reading burden's near adjourned;—
I'd be remiss to—as a former teacher—
Neglect to analyze what I have learned
In studying—(with love!)—the male creature.
A yellow jacket stung me on the ear:—
For two whole weeks, the venom in my veins
Seemed with my arms' healing to interfere;—
Infected blood normality constrains.
My move from patient to trainee, likewise,
Seemed to enthrall two streams,—flirting impel;—
But love was gushing in aberrant guise:—
The diff'rence is, the prick followed the spell!
You don't get paid to touch up faded me:—
True love is unbewitched,—nontoxic,—free.

Sonnet 153

Full moon's icumin in! O bright December!
I'll—star—this second finding contemplate:
As faded you, my friend said, "L, remember,
You're awesome!—vivid, right? You shouldn't wait.
A satellite's a martyr,—which seems nice;—
Most planets like a constant ringlet. But:—
You'll wane past crescent;—wasting won't entice
Your flame to stargaze,—just you undercut.
And:—playing hard-to-get's reverse poor form,—
A far-off, cold, unfathomable show.
The best move is:—be visible and warm,
While—vigorously—you pick up and go!"
That's why, from you, my blazing starship sped:—
Why—astronaut—you're burning up my bed!

Sonnet 154

The troubadour on courtly love's obsessin',—
His love to Laura Petrarch keeps professin',—
To his Dark Lady Shakespeare's still confessin',—
As I sing you this third and final lesson:
When for love unattainable one longs,
It's helpful to express oneself in songs;—
When one's belov'd—or crosséd stars—one wrongs,
One's crazed, fanatic hurt in verse belongs.
But when your kisses steal my ache forlorn,—
When you for sweet, long days my life adorn,—
When waking 'side you feels like Xmas morn,—
That's when one sets aside the old inkhorn.
How 'bout, next time I think on you—(ho sexy!)—
Instead of hustlin' rhymes,—I call or text ye?

Sonnet 155

How bittersweet is, Will, a chapbook's end;—
Wassup, great sonneteer of long ago?
In this fast-wrapping space-time, I'll expend
A few breaths on your brilliant, long shadow:
Methinks, in your own way, my life you saved,—
As did, their ways, the other two address
I in these verses:—as tough times I braved,
You freed me with your talents and finesse.
Your virtuosity astounds me;—I,
Bard, hereby dedicate this book to you!
So many sonnets light and scale your sky,—
But, as we humans judge, can it be true?—
This glaring fact we really can't ignore:—
You only wrote one hundred fifty-four. . . .

Some of the sonnets in this collection were first published in literary journals, sometimes in a slightly different form. Sonnets 129 and 130 first appeared in *Beltway Poetry Quarterly*. Sonnet 114 first appeared in *The Headlight Review*. Sonnets 122, 123, and 127 first appeared in *Tofu Ink Arts Press*, Volume 4. Sonnets 35, 39, and 42 first appeared in *Brief Wilderness*. Sonnets 121 and 124 first appeared in *The Big Windows Review*. Sonnets 41, 45, and 51 first appeared in *Burrow*. Sonnets 12, 21, 31, 38, 43, and 54 first appeared in *Exacting Clam*.

ACKNOWLEDGMENTS

Endless thanks to the three men I address in these sonnets. Without you, obviously, . . . none of this. Thank you to those who read and commented on the manuscript, in particular (in alphabetical order) Mary Dempsey, Kteba Dunlap, Kevin Harris, Mary Roberson, Gina Robinson, and Bob Wachholder. Thank you to Indran Amirthanayagam for inviting me to read sonnets at Poetry at the Port, submit sonnets to *Beltway Poetry Quarterly*, and submit the full manuscript to Beltway Editions. Thank you to all of the editors of literary journals who accepted sonnets for publication. Thank you to Indran Amirthanayagam, Sara Cahill Marron, and everyone at Beltway Editions for publishing this book. Thank you to Jorge Ureta Sandoval for graphic design. Thank you to John D. Mason for legal counsel. And much gratitude to my family and friends for your love and support.

Liza Achilles

has contributed poetry and nonfiction to *Beltway Poetry Quarterly*, *The Headlight Review*, *Tofu Ink Arts Press*, *Brief Wilderness*, *The Big Windows Review*, *Burrow*, *Exacting Clam*, the *Washington Independent Review of Books*, the Silent Book Club blog, and independent blogs. Her blog at lizaachilles.com is about the literary world, present and past, literary fiction and nonfiction and poetry. She lives in the Washington, DC, area.

Author photo: Clay Blackmore

TWO NOVEMBERS

PRINTING WAS COMPLETED IN FEBRUARY 2024 FOR **Beltway Editions**